Daily Life

by Grace Hansen

Abdo
DISCOVERING
ANCIENT EGYPT
Kids

Abdo Kids Jumbo is an Imprint of Abdo Kids
abdobooks.com

abdobooks.com

Published by Abdo Kids, a division of ABDO, P.O. Box 398166, Minneapolis, Minnesota 55439.
Copyright © 2024 by Abdo Consulting Group, Inc. International copyrights reserved in all countries.
No part of this book may be reproduced in any form without written permission from the publisher.
Abdo Kids Jumbo™ is a trademark and logo of Abdo Kids.

Printed in the United States of America, North Mankato, Minnesota.

102023

012024

THIS BOOK CONTAINS
RECYCLED MATERIALS

Photo Credits: Alamy, Getty Images, Shutterstock

Production Contributors: Teddy Borth, Jennie Forsberg, Grace Hansen
Design Contributors: Victoria Bates, Candice Keimig

Library of Congress Control Number: 2023937694
Publisher's Cataloging-in-Publication Data

Names: Hansen, Grace, author.
Title: Daily life / by Grace Hansen
Description: Minneapolis, Minnesota : Abdo Kids, 2024 | Series: Discovering ancient Egypt | Includes
    online resources and index.
Identifiers: ISBN 9781098268435 (lib. bdg.) | ISBN 9781098269135 (ebook) | ISBN 9781098269487
    (Read-to-Me ebook)
Subjects: LCSH: History, Ancient--Juvenile literature. | Egypt--Civilization--Juvenile literature. |
    Anthropology--Juvenile literature.
Classification: DDC 932--dc23

OCTOBER 2024

Table of Contents

A Day in the Life

The ancient Egyptians enjoyed daily life. They worked, played, got married, and cared for pets.

4

5

Home

Most ancient Egyptians lived in simple homes. These homes were made of mud mixed with straw or sand to form bricks. Doors were made of **papyrus**.

Jobs & Education

Most Egyptians worked hard every day. There were many different jobs. Every skill was considered important. Women often sewed, cooked, and managed households.

8

9

Men were often farmers, fishermen, or potters. Some became soldiers. Men from any job could be called to build pyramids. Both men and women could be musicians or dancers.

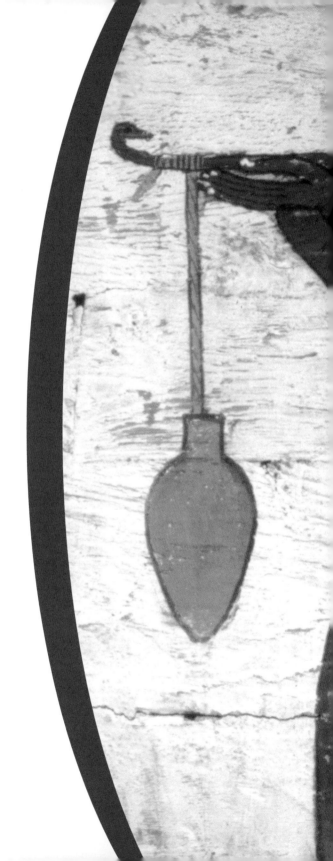

Most boys and girls did not go to school. They learned religion and practical life skills. At age 14, boys began working as **apprentices** or with their fathers.

Farming & Food

The ancient Egyptians created an **irrigation** system. It carried water from the Nile River to farmland. The **staple crops** were wheat and barley. These were used to make bread and drinks.

14

15

Wealthy Egyptians often ate fruits and vegetables. Cows, sheep, ducks, and other animals were sources of protein.

Clothing & Accessories

Most ancient Egyptians wore clothing made of linen. They sometimes colored the cloth yellow, red, or blue.

19

Both men and women wore makeup, perfume, and jewelry. Jewelry often had symbols meant to protect the person wearing it.

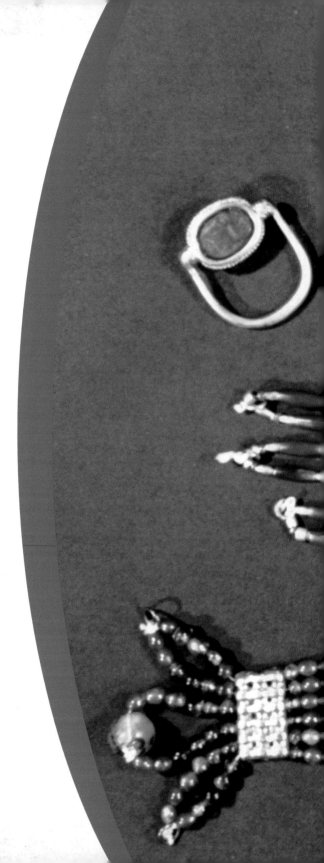

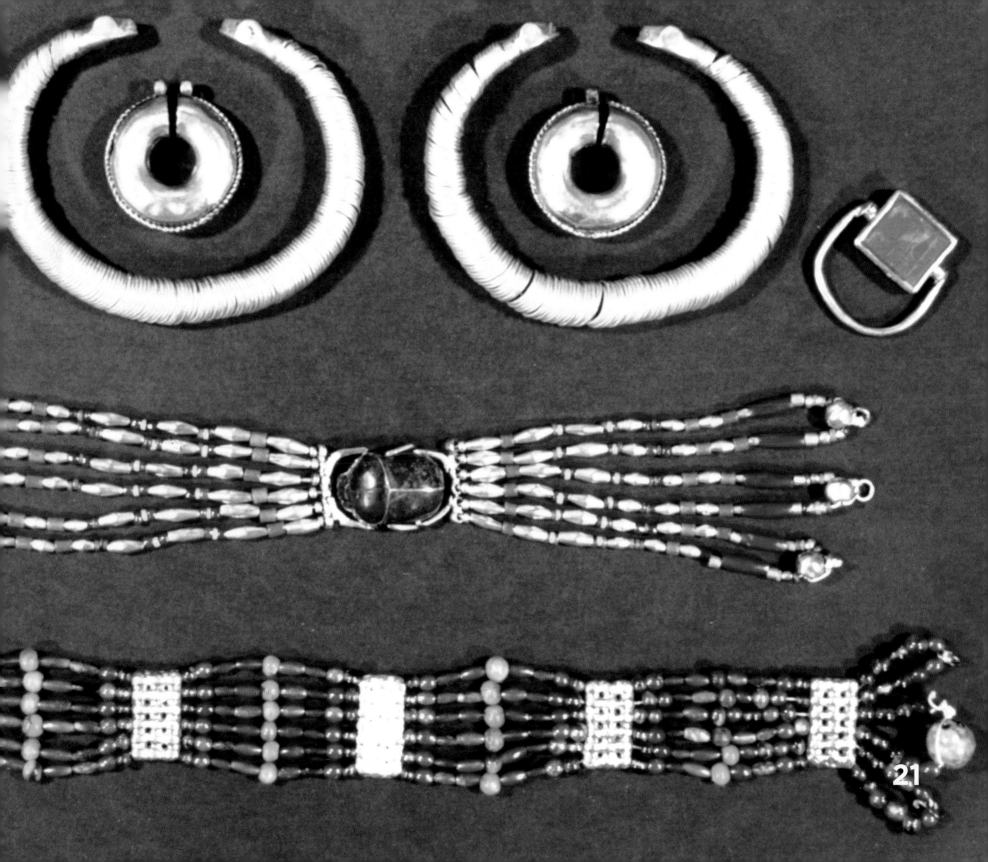

21

Ancient Egyptian Pets

cats

Many ancient Egyptians enjoyed having pets. Some animals were considered **sacred** such as cats, dogs, and certain birds.

dogs

birds

monkeys

gazelles

Glossary

apprentice – someone who works for somebody else to learn that person's skill or trade.

irrigation – the supply of water to land by man-made means.

papyrus – a tall water plant of the Nile valley in Egypt.

protein – a substance that is found in all living things and are a necessary part of life processes.

sacred – considered holy and deserving respect, especially because of a connection with a god.

staple crop – one of a region's most important crops, typically making up a major portion of a region's diet.

Index

Abdo Kids
ONLINE
FREE! ONLINE MULTIMEDIA RESOURCES

Visit **abdokids.com**
to access crafts, games,
videos, and more!

Use Abdo Kids code
DDK8435
or scan this QR code!